Mimi Pond's

Secrets of the

Powder Room

Mimi Pond's
Secrets of the Powder Room

What Every MAN Should Know About Women

HOLT, RINEHART AND WINSTON · NEW YORK · AN OWL BOOK

SOME OF THIS MATERIAL HAS APPEARED IN
DIFFERENT FORM IN **THE VILLAGE VOICE.**
COPYRIGHT © 1983 BY MIMI POND
ALL RIGHTS RESERVED, INCLUDING THE RIGHT TO REPRODUCE
THIS BOOK OR PORTIONS THEREOF IN ANY FORM.
PUBLISHED BY HOLT, RINEHART AND WINSTON, 383 MADISON AVENUE,
NEW YORK, NEW YORK 10017.
PUBLISHED SIMULTANEOUSLY IN CANADA BY HOLT, RINEHART
AND WINSTON OF CANADA, LIMITED.

LIBRARY OF CONGRESS CATALOGING IN PUBLICATION DATA
POND, MIMI.
MIMI POND'S SECRETS OF THE POWDER ROOM.
1. WOMEN—CARICATURES AND CARTOONS. I. TITLE
PN6 727. P66 W5   1983   741.5'973   84-4323
ISBN 0-03-063253-6

FIRST EDITION
PRINTED IN THE UNITED STATES OF AMERICA
1 3 5 7 9 10 8 6 4 2

THE BIG DIFFERENCES BETWEEN MEN AND WOMEN

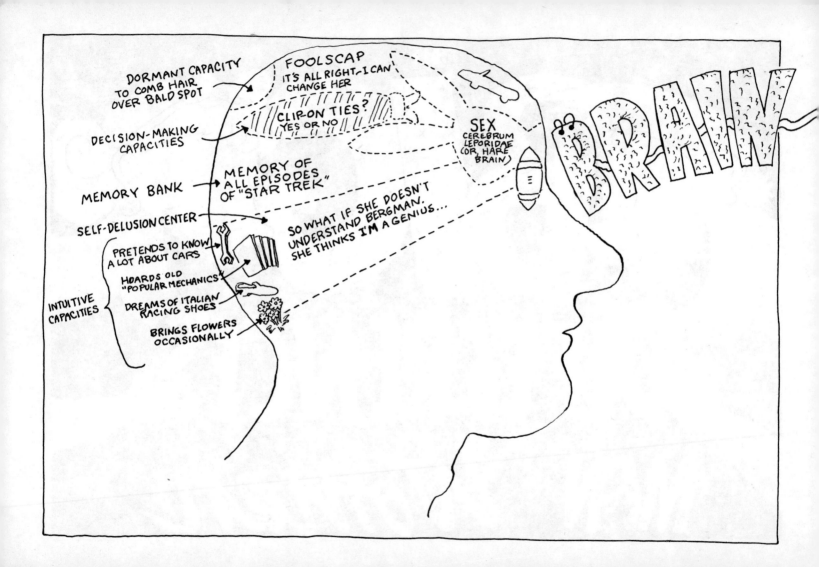

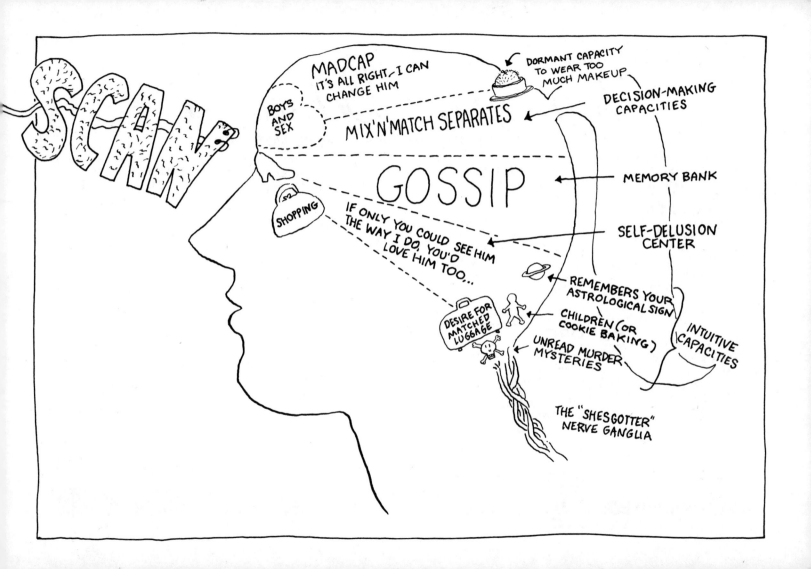

THE BIG DIFFERENCES BETWEEN MEN and Women

MEN: HAVE REALLY UGLY MISMATCHED SHEETS.

I LIKE EVERYTHING ABOUT YOU EXCEPT FOR ONE THING.

WHAT?

YOUR "SMURF" SHEETS.

MEN: ALWAYS LOOK TO SEE WHAT'S IN THE REFRIGERATOR.

MEN: ALWAYS HIDE THEIR COPY OF "PLAYBOY."

READING SOMETHING? ME? NO, WHY DO YOU ASK?

WOMEN: HAVE NICE MATCHING DESIGNER SHEETS.

OH, BOO, HOO, HOO!

WHY DARLING, HAVE I NOT SATISFIED YOU?

HOW **COULD** I COME WHEN YOU DIDN'T EVEN NOTICE MY NEW GLORIA VANDERBILT SHEETS?

WOMEN: ALWAYS SNOOP IN BATHROOM CABINETS.

WHITE SHOULDERS—I SHOULD'VE GUESSED. I'LL BET SHE'LL NEVER MISS THAT LIPGLOSS...

WOMEN: ARE NOT ASHAMED OF HAVING THEIR COPY OF "COSMOPOLITAN" IN PLAIN SIGHT, EVEN THOUGH THEY SHOULD BE.

HONEY! THIS ARTICLE SAYS THE SIZE OF YOUR PENIS IS LINKED TO YOUR ASTROLOGICAL SIGN!

WHAT WOMEN Really

1. SENTIMENTAL TICKET STUBS FROM TEN YEARS AGO
2. THIS YEAR'S APPOINTMENT CALENDAR
3. LAST YEAR'S APPOINTMENT CALENDAR, TO COMPARE POPULARITY
4. BANANA YOGURT
5. 12 PAIR PANTYHOSE
6. COTTON BALLS
7. CORDLESS TELEPHONE
8. EXTRA PAIR PUMPS FOR EMERGENCY FORMAL OCCASION
9. EMERGENCY PACK OF NINETY-SIX TAMPONS
10. COMBINED MAKE-UP AND EXECTROLYSIS LABORATORY
11. BIRTH CONTROL
12. SMALL MIRROR
13. GIANT FRAMED PHOTO OF OLD BOYFRIEND
14. ROLODEX OF OLD BOYFRIENDS
15. ENORMOUS PUFFBALL KEYCHAIN

Women ARE SOCIALIZED TO DEVELOP THEIR INTUITIVE QUALITIES FAR MORE THAN MEN. OFTEN THEY CAN HOLD CONVERSATIONS THAT SEEM CONFUSING TO THE OPPOSITE SEX. HOWEVER, IF YOU LEARN TO "HEAR BETWEEN THE LINES," YOU'LL HAVE A MUCH BETTER UNDERSTANDING OF WOMEN.

LOVELY HAT! NEW?

GEORGE? THE SNOW TIRES?

MM-HM—KNOW WHY?

MORE OR LESS.

REALLY I CAN'T SEE WHY...

WELL YOU KNOW THE WAY GEORGE...

I KNOW, I KNOW...

AND THE CHAINSAW, **THAT** WAS THE LIMIT.

BUT DORIS AND HER **ELECTROLUX**...

I REMEMBER, GOD KNOWS...

GEORGE IS THE HUSBAND OF THE WOMAN IN THE NEW HAT. HE IS IMPOTENT EXCEPT FOR RIGHT AFTER HE PUTS THE SNOW TIRES ON THE CAR. HE FEELS GUILTY AND HAS BOUGHT HIS WIFE A NEW HAT. DORIS HAS A SIMILAR PROBLEM: SHE IS FRIGID EXCEPT

WHAT ABOUT FELIX?

ANCHORAGE. THE ROCKETTES. **COMPLETELY** CONFUSED.

HOW SAD FOR MAUREEN.

WORSE STILL FOR THE KIDS.

ALL THAT WORK, AND FOR NOTHING.

FOR WHEN SHE VACUUMS. FELIX IS THE WOMAN ON THE RIGHT'S BROTHER. HE FLED TO ALASKA AFTER A SCANDAL INVOLVING THE ROCKETTES, THE "KIDS" ARE HIS GOAT-HERD HE HAS BEEN RAISING — NOW ABANDONED. THE WOMAN ON THE LEFT OWNS 40% OF

40%

NEW FROCK?

GOOD WORK— BENDEL'S?

BLOOMIE'S— BUT—

DOMINIQUE?

MM-HM, BUT **PUCE**..

OF COURSE. REALLY, **YELLOW**. IT'S PREPOSTEROUS.

HER NEW DRESS. THE OTHER 60% BELONGS TO HER SISTER, DOMINIQUE. THEY HAD AN ARGUMENT OVER WHICH COLOR TO BUY. HARDLY ANYONE CAN WEAR YELLOW. CERTAINLY **NOT** DOMINIQUE...

THE SECRET OF The Powder Room

ALL WOMEN HAVE... PREGNANCY ANXIETY

HI, SHIRLEY? IT'S DORETTA. LISTEN I THINK I'M P.G.!

OH, GEE, HONEY, WHEN WAS YOUR PERIOD DUE?

IN TWO WEEKS — I THINK MY TITS ARE GETTING BIGGER!

WHAT'RE YOU **WORRIED** ABOUT? DIDN'T YOU USE YOUR DIAPHRAGM?

WELL, YEAH, BUT IT WAS AN OLD TUBE OF JELLY. IT EXPIRED THREE DAYS AGO!

WAS THAT THREE DAYS AGO **TODAY** OR THREE DAYS RIGHT **AFTER** YOU DID IT?

IF YOU KNEW HOW WE WORRIED, YOU WOULDN'T WANT TO TAKE THESE CHANCES.

JUST THIS ONCE, BABY, C'MON...

LET'S SEE... IT'S DAY 17, AND YOU'RE MOST FERTILE RIGHT **BEFORE** YOUR PERIOD—NO, RIGHT **AFTER**, BUT THIS IS THE MIDDLE, AND...

OH GEE...

SOMETIMES IT'S AN **UNREASONABLE** FEAR...

OH PHYLLIS, I THINK I'M **PREGNANT**!

BUT YOU HAVEN'T GOTTEN LAID IN **MONTHS**.

I KNOW, BUT IT COULD BE **DORMANT**.

...BUT ALWAYS MAKE SURE YOU PROCEED WITH **CAUTION**.

DON'T **WORRY**, HONEY. YOU'VE GOT THE DIAPHRAGM, I'VE GOT A RUBBER, WE'RE USING FOAM, AND I'M GOING TO WITHDRAW...

WELL...**OKAY**, BUT YOU HAVE TO TELL ME YOU LOVE ME WHEN YOU COME.

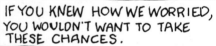
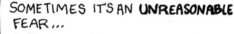

THE PRACTICE SESSION

WOMEN GRAVE

HELLO #1: ALL BUSINESS.

HELLO.

HELLO #2: BORED.

YES?

HELLO #3: FEMININE.

HELLO? ♪

HELLO #4: FRIENDLY.

HOWDY-DO!

HMMM...

THE REAL THING:

R-R-RING!

PHONE CALLS

What Women Really Want

"NO! I WANT TO WATCH SPORTS AND DRINK BEER!"

Panel 1

WOMEN ARE THOROUGHLY FAMILIAR WITH THE RITES OF SHOPPING.

"I'LL COVER SPORTSWEAR, YOU HANDLE LINGERIE, I'LL MEET YOU IN SMALL LEATHER GOODS AT 1400 HOURS."

"CHECK! SYNCHRONIZE WATCHES!"

Panel 2

MEN HAVE NOT BEEN TRAINED THIS WAY. THEY BECOME **DISORIENTED** EASILY...

"SIT DOWN!"

"BUT ALL I WANTED WAS **SOCKS!**"

"NONSENSE. YOU'RE HERE FOR A COMPLETE **MAKE-OVER!**"

Panel 3

...WHICH IS WHY THEY **NEED** WOMEN TO GUIDE THEM THROUGH "DANGEROUS" TERRITORY.

ELECTRONIC-STEREOS-TVS-VIDEO

"L-L-LOOK, HONEY! **STEREO** EQUIPMENT!"

"FIDDLE FADDLE! YOU'RE GOING TO HELP ME LOOK AT **HATS!**"

Panel 4

BUT WOMEN NEED **YOUR** MORAL SUPPORT AS THEY SHOP.

"DOESN'T IT JUST HAVE MY NAME **WRITTEN** ALL OVER IT?"

SHOPPING

YOU GO SHOPPING WITH THEM!

COME **ON**, HONEY, THERE'S A SALE AND WE CAN EAT LUNCH IN A CUTE PLACE!

PRACTICE SUCH PHRASES AS **THESE**:

OH DEAR IT'S LOVELY.

DO YOU **REALLY** THINK SO?

⑤

THAT DRESS IS YOU.

THAT'S WHAT I SAID. I SAID, "THELMA, THAT DRESS IS YOU!"

⑥

TACT IS EVERYTHING...

I DON'T KNOW **WHY** THIS SIZE 14 DOESN'T FIT ME...

WHY DEAR, THESE ARE **EUROPEAN** SIZES. THEY RUN SMALL.

⑦

THERE **ARE** A FEW SIDE BENEFITS...

MAY I **HELP** YOU, SIR?

WELL, SHUCKS...

ANYTHING WE COULD... **SHOW** YOU?

WHY YOU...

⑧

CLOTHES THAT GIRLS DON'T LIKE!
PLAID PANTS
White Shoes
I'D RATHER BE SKIING
GOOFY HATS
W-I-D-E T-I-E-S
OPEN-TO-THE-WAIST NYLON ACETATE SPORT SHIRTS

A Woman and Her Lingerie

SHERE HITE SAYS WOMEN RARELY ORGASM. SO MEN WANT TO KNOW, "WHY DO THEY KEEP GOING TO BED?" ONE COULD SAY THAT IT IS THE KNOWLEDGE THAT THEY WILL EVENTUALLY GET TO SLEEP, BUT THIS IS OVER-SIMPLIFICATION. WOMEN HAVE AN INHERENT NEED FOR MEN TO ADMIRE THEIR UNDERWEAR.

THEY **COULD** SHOW IT OFF TO THEIR GIRL FRIENDS, BUT AS ANY WOMAN CAN TELL YOU, **IT'S NOT THE SAME.**

SO, WHADDAYA THINK?

OH-YEAH. YOU STILL WANT TO GO TO THE MALL?

FOUNDATION GARMENTS ARE 90% OF FOREPLAY, WHICH IS SIMPLY ANOTHER VERSION OF "HIDE-AND-GO-SEEK."

WHAT DO I SPY HERE? **BLACK LACE?** YOU **VIXEN!**

REMEMBER, THE **SOLE** REASON THAT A WOMAN WEARS A GARTER BELT IS BECAUSE IT MAKES HER FEEL **NASTY.**

OH, YOU **DIRTY, DIRTY GIRL!**

SHE PAID ONE-QUARTER OF LAST WEEK'S PAYCHECK FOR THOSE SKIMPY LITTLE ITEMS, AND **ALL FOR YOU.** ADMIRE THAT UNDERWEAR!

BLACK LACE! DO YOU KNOW WHAT THAT **DOES** TO A MAN?

NO, WHAT? TEEHEE!

GET DOWN ON YOUR HANDS AND KNEES AND **WORSHIP** THAT UNDERWEAR! AND WHILE YOU'RE DOWN THERE...

YOU **TEMPTRESS!** YOU **RAVISHING CREATURE!** DO YOU **KNOW** WHAT I'M GOING TO **DO** TO YOU **NOW?**

I CAN ONLY **HOPE...**

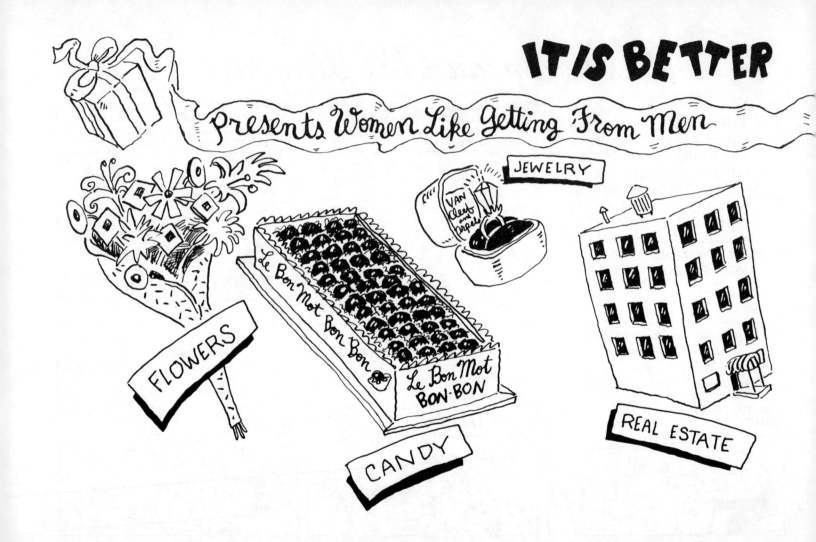

TO GIVE!

Presents Women Could Do Without

A BOTTLE OF CHAMPALE

Champale

PLEXIGLAS ICE-SCRAPER

"SKEETER SKAT"

ELECTRIC MOSQUITO REPELLANT

A TUPPERWARE STARTER SET WITH LETTUCE CRISPER BONUS!

NEW YORK ISLANDERS VS NEW JERSEY SLEAZOIDS

HOCKEY TICKETS!

Women Love Endearing Terms

HONEY BUNNY!

DUCKBUMPS!

WOMEN ADORE FOR THEIR MEN TO CALL THEM BY FOND AND DOTING NAMES. IF YOU'RE NOT FROM THE SOUTHERN HALF OF THE UNITED STATES, YOU MAY BE UNFAMILIAR WITH THESE WORDS, GUARANTEED TO MELT THE **COLDEST** OF HEARTS.

SUGARS
SUGAR LUMP
SUGAR SWEET
SUGAR BABY
(MY LITTLE)
SUGAR-PLUM FAIRY

PIES
HONEY PIE
SUGAR PIE
PEACH PIE
LAMB PIE
CUTEY PIE
PUDDING PIE
SWEET-POTATO-PIE

FLOWERS
PEACH BLOSSOM
PLUM BLOSSOM
APPLE BLOSSOM
FLOWER BABY
SWEET-PEA
ROSEBUD

FRUITS AND VEGETABLES
MY LITTLE:
MUSKMELON
CABBAGE (CHOU-CHOU)
CANTALOUPE
POMEGRANATE
PAPAYA
PUMPKIN

HONEYS
HONEY BUNCH
HONEY LAMB
HONEY BUNNY

DOLLS
DOLL FACE
DOLL BABY

MINERALS
MY-PEARL-BEYOND PRICE
MY GEM
MY JEWEL

ANIMALS
BUNNY
LAMBIE
KITTEN
DUCKIE
DUCKBUMPS
HUSH PUPPY

NONSENSE
BOO-BOO
BUN-BUNS
WOOGIE
PEE-PIE

OTHER DESSERTS
CUPCAKE
LOLLIPOP
CREAMPUFF
CREAMCHEESE
COOKIE

GENERIC
HEART-OF-HEARTS
SWEETHEART
DARLING
KID
ANGELFACE

YOU CAN MAKE CHARMING COMBINATIONS OF MANY OF THESE WORDS, SUCH AS THE FAMOUS "SUGARPIE HONEYBUNCH," "APPLEBLOSSOM DOLLBABY," OR EVEN "LAMBIEFACE."

FLATTERY WILL GET YOU *Anywhere!*

WOMEN THE WORLD OVER ARE WAITING FOR YOU TO FLATTER THEM.

WHERE IS HE?

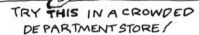

TRY **THIS** IN A CROWDED DEPARTMENT STORE!

WHAT IS THAT SCENT YOU'RE WEARING?

OH... DO YOU LIKE IT?

A SIMPLE PHRASE LIKE THIS WILL PUT **YOU** IN THE DRIVER'S SEAT!

YOU REMIND ME OF SUZANNE PLESHETTE AT HER PEAK.

BUT THERE'S THE VIVACITY OF BRITT EKLAND FROM HER "IF THIS IS TUESDAY THIS MUST BE BELGIUM" PERIOD...

TAKE ME AWAY!

THE WORLD GOES 'ROUND ON LITTLE WHITE LIES.

EYES LIKE A YOUNG SPRINGBOK...

TELL ME MORE.

CURBSIDE ETIQUETTE

WRONG

WOMEN **LOATHE** THIS CHILDISH PRACTICE.

RIGHT

A DISPLAY OF **SINCERE** ENTHUSIASM IS **WELCOMED** BY WOMEN OF DISCRIMINATING TASTES.

GOOD PLACES

TO MEET WOMEN

Good Ways to Get a Woman's Attention

A Quiz

DESPERATE DATING ATTEMPTS

Why They Don't Work

CLASSIFIED ADS:

YOU **COULD** MEET THE RIGHT TYPE— **IF** YOU HAPPEN TO BE FREDERICO FELLINI'S CASTING AGENT...

ATTRACTIVE SINGLE FEMALE, ENJOYS WALKS ON BEACH, SUNSETS, "GENERAL HOSPITAL," SEX, INTO "WORKING ON HERSELF" AND BEING IN TOUCH W/COSMOS. BOX 77034,

COMPUTER DATING:

ABOUT THE SAME—NOT **TOO** MUCH DIFFERENT FROM STICKING YOUR TOOL THROUGH A HOLE IN THE FENCE.

COMPUTER DATING
SERVICE QUESTIONNAIRE

① I: Ⓐ LIKE ENEMAS ☐
   Ⓑ HATE ENEMAS ☐
② I: Ⓐ LIKE TUINOLS ☐
   Ⓑ HATE TUINOLS ☐
③ I: Ⓐ LIKE SEX ☐
   Ⓑ HATE SEX ☐
   I: Ⓐ LIKE THE SME
④ OF MY OWN FAR
   I: Ⓑ LIKE THE SM
   OF OTHERS' FA

SINGLES BARS:

GOOD PLACES TO MEET WOMEN WHO'VE DECORATED THEIR APARTMENTS COMPLETELY IN YELLOW.

MADAME **BOVARY**? THAT WAS THE CHARACTER DOLLY PARTON PLAYED IN "BEST LITTLE WHOREHOUSE IN TEXAS," RIGHT?

DEALING WITH REJECTION

DON'T: WRITE HER NAME AND NUMBER ON BATHROOM WALLS!

FOR A GOOD TIME CALL SHEIL

DON'T: EMBARRASS HER IN FRONT OF HER FRIENDS AND FAMILY.

WHO IS THIS YOUNG MAN, DEAR?

NO ONE, REALLY, MOTHER.

I STAND ACCUSED! I WANT YOU BACK! I CAN'T HELP MYSELF! WHAT DOES IT TAKE TO WIN YOUR LOVE? WHAT BECOMES OF THE BROKEN HEARTED? WHY DO FOOLS FALL IN LOVE? MY WHOLE WORLD ENDED! I HEARD IT THROUGH THE GRAPEVINE! BABY I NEE

DO: THINK ABOUT HOW **SORRY** SHE'D BE IF YOU WERE DEAD. SELF-PITY IS A NATURAL BY-PRODUCT OF REJECTION.

I SHOULD'VE GONE OUT WITH HIM!

R.I.P. "SHE DIDN'T LIKE ME"

DO: DATE OTHERS.

SO, THIS GIRL I MET, SHE WAS SO **BEAUTIFUL**, LONG BLOND HAIR, A FIGURE LIKE YOU WOULDN'T BELIEVE— SHE WOULDN'T GO OUT WITH ME— I CAN'T FIGURE IT OUT. I'M A NICE GUY, RIGHT?

I GUESS.

DO: TALK ABOUT IT WITH YOUR FRIENDS.

SHE WOULDN'T EVEN **GO OUT** WITH ME! I DON'T THINK SHE **LIKED** ME— HOW COULD THAT **BE**? WHY **WOULDN'T** SHE LIKE ME? **YOU** LIKE ME, RIGHT, BOB?

ZZZZ

TAKE A Hint?

WOMEN ARE COMPLEX CREATURES CAPABLE OF STRANGE SUBTLETIES THAT OFTEN ESCAPE MEN...

AT A PARTY...

GOSH, I SEE YOU'RE WEARING **LEATHER PANTS** TOO. I THINK LEATHER IS **SO SENSUOUS**...

I ALWAYS WONDERED WHAT WOULD HAPPEN IF TWO PEOPLE WEARING LEATHER PANTS STARTED **RUBBING** AGAINST EACH OTHER. I MEAN, WOULD THEY **STICK TOGETHER**? WOULD THERE BE **STATIC CLING**? DO YOU THINK IT WOULD SWEAT?

GEE. I DON'T KNOW. DO YOU KNOW WHERE THEY KEEP THE ICE?

Q U E S T I O N S

① IS THIS WOMAN JUST MAKING "PLEASANT CHATTER"?

② IS SHE JUST TRYING TO MAKE OTHER GUESTS FEEL "AT EASE"?

③ SHE PROBABLY IS JUST TRYING TO BE "POLITE," RIGHT?

④ IS THE MAN GAY, OR IS HE JUST STUPID?

IF YOU ANSWERED "**NO**" TO QUESTIONS **1, 2,** AND **3** AND "**YES**" TO QUESTION **4,** YOU HAVE A REFINED SENSE OF INTUITION. IF YOU **DIDN'T,** YOU PROBABLY NEED **MORE** THAN THIS BOOK HAS TO OFFER.

HOW TO MAKE WOMEN NERVOUS

WOMEN LIKE TO BE MADE NERVOUS. IT THROWS THEM OFF-BALANCE. THIS SENSATION OF CONFUSION MAKES THEM THINK THAT THEY ARE IN **LOVE** WITH YOU.

STEP ONE: WEAR A **REALLY** NICE SUIT. THIS WILL MAKE HER THINK YOU DON'T NEED HER.

NICE SUIT! WONDER WHO HELPED HIM PICK IT OUT?

STEP TWO: WEAR A SHIRT WITH FRENCH CUFFS AND MONOGRAMS.

A MONOGRAM! WOW! WHAT CLASS!

STEP THREE: DISPLAY EXQUISITE MANNERS.

LET ME HELP YOU WITH YOUR COAT... WH-WH-WHAT?

STEP FOUR: SEE HER TO HER DOOR.

I HAD A LOVELY TIME, I'VE GOT TO CATCH A TRAIN, I'LL CALL YOU.

YOU DID? YOU DO? YOU WILL?

STEP FIVE: WAIT TWO WEEKS BEFORE CALLING HER AGAIN. REPEAT PROCESS SEVERAL TIMES.

JUNE

TICK TICK TICK TICK TICK TICK TICK

PLAYING COY

PLAYING "COY" IS EASY—PRACTICE THESE PHRASES AND EXPRESSIONS BEFORE A MIRROR.

OH, I BET YOU SAY THAT TO **ALL** THE MEN, MISS SMITH!

WAG WAG

WHEN SHE SAYS SOMETHING SERIOUS AND INTELLIGENT, SAY THIS:

GOSH!

HERE'S A GOOD EXPRESSION FOR THOSE "QUIET MOMENTS."

EVENTUALLY YOUR DATE WILL ASK A DIRECT QUESTION...

TELL ME—DO YOU FIND ME... ATTRACTIVE?

ANSWERING COYLY WILL DRIVE HER WILD WITH DESIRE.

WHY, WHATEVER DO YOU MEAN?

RRROW!!

HIDDEN SIGNALS

EVER WONDER IF A WOMAN WAS SENDING YOU SIGNALS FROM ACROSS THE ROOM? HERE'S HOW TO TELL A "COME HITHER" FROM A "BEAT IT, BUB!"

WHEN YOU'RE SITTING NEARBY, SHE MAY START SPEAKING MORE LOUDLY TO HER GIRLFRIEND.

THIS IS A "HINT" THAT SHE WOULD LIKE TO GET YOUR ATTENTION.

WITHOUT EVEN TALKING TO YOU, SHE CAN LET YOU KNOW THAT SHE'S INTERESTED.

REMEMBER TO SMILE...

...BUT TRUST YOUR INTUITIONS.

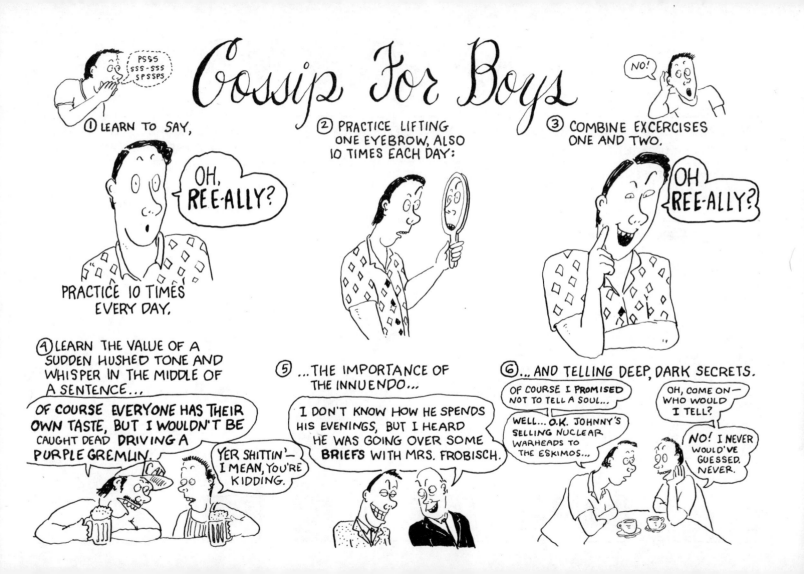

What's your  **CLOTHING**

CONSCIOUSNESS?

IT DOESN'T HAVE TO BE MUCH...

I LIKE TO SEE A WOMAN IN A PEPLUM, OF COURSE, I'M **MAD** ABOUT RETRO...

...IN FACT, IF YOU'RE TOO WELL INFORMED ABOUT WOMEN'S CLOTHES YOU MAY BE SUSPECT.

I WAS ABSOLUTELY **STUNNED** BY THE ARMANI COLLECTION I SAW IN MILAN THIS FALL—OF COURSE THE JAPANESE ARE REALLY—WELL LOOK AT KENZO—I MEAN **PLEASE.**

UH-HUH. AND HOW DO YOU FEEL ABOUT JUDY GARLAND?

THEY FIND YOUR MINOR KNOWLEDGE OF FASHION AS CHARMING AS YOU FIND THEIR KNOWLEDGE OF SPORTS. SOME REALMS ARE BETTER LEFT UNTOUCHED...

WHAT FETCHING **TOREADOR** PANTS, DEAR!

THEY'RE **JODHPURS**—ARE WE GOING TO YOUR LITTLE BASEBALL GAME TOMORROW?

IT'S THE **SUPERBOWL,** MY PET!

Billets-Doux

HOW **YOU** CAN TELL THE DIFFERENCE BETWEEN...

Miss Right and *MISS WRONG*

QUALITIES

1. BATHES OFTEN.
2. LIKES TO WATCH RERUNS OF "HAWAII 5-0."
3. GETS UP AND MAKES THE COFFEE.
4. DOESN'T GET SLOPPY DRUNK.
5. ISN'T FLAT-CHESTED.
6. LIKES TO DO "IT" WHEN **I** WANT TO.

IS SHE RIGHT FOR ME?

7. WILL NOT THROW MY TURNTABLE ACROSS THE ROOM IN A JEALOUS RAGE.
8. DOESN'T HAVE A DOG.
9. WILL NOT GAIN 25 POUNDS AFTER I MOVE IN.
10. WILL NOT CRY WHEN I FORGET HER BIRTHDAY.
11. HAS A JOB EVEN WHEN I DON'T.

Where to meet Miss Right?

- AT A METHODIST YOUTH FELLOWSHIP CONFERENCE
- AT YOUR PARENTS' HOUSE
- AT REX HUMBARD BIBLE COLLEGE

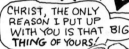

QUALITIES

1. WANTS TO DO "IT" ALL THE TIME.
2. MOUTH HANGS OPEN.
3. LIKES TO WATCH "THE NEWLYWED GAME."
4. OFFENDS MY FRIENDS.
5. WEARS NO UNDERWEAR.
6. HAS ENORMOUS BREASTS.

IS SHE WRONG FOR ME?

7. TALKS BABY TALK.
8. ILLITERATE.
9. HAS A BIG, JEALOUS BOYFRIEND.
10. GETS SLOPPY DRUNK.
11. LIKES TO TAKE OFF ALL HER CLOTHES IN PUBLIC.
12. WILL CALL MY MOTHER AT 3 A.M. TO COMPLAIN ABOUT ME.

Where to meet Miss Wrong?

- AT A CONCERT OF "THE SLITS"
- IN A MASSAGE PARLOR
- AT A HELL'S ANGELS' CONVENTION

LAFFS 'N' LIBIDOS!

WOMEN FIND MEN WHO HAVE A SENSE OF HUMOR **EXTREMELY SEXY!** YOU DON'T HAVE TO LOOK LIKE ROBERT REDFORD. ALL YOU HAVE TO DO IS TICKLE HER FUNNY BONE, AND SHE'LL FOLLOW YOU ANYWHERE!

FAMOUS ARTISTS SCHOOL!

Make-Out

RULE # 1

WOMEN LOVE TO MAKE OUT! IF YOU WANT TO MAKE HER HAPPY, YOU'LL SPEND AT LEAST **THREE HOURS** LIP-WRESTLING ON THE SOFA. IF YOU GET BORED, HERE'S SOME LITTLE MENTAL GAMES TO KEEP YOURSELF ALERT AND ON THE JOB!

- MENTALLY BALANCE YOUR CHECKBOOK!
- IN YOUR MIND, TAKE APART AND RECONSTRUCT YOUR CAR'S TRANSMISSION!
- TRY TO REMEMBER ALL THE STATES IN THE UNION!

FUN with Birth Control

I.U.D.

STANDS FOR INTER-UTERINE DEVICE. A PIECE OF METAL THAT THE DOCTOR INSERTS "UP THERE." IMAGINE THAT SHE HAS A SMALL T.V. ANTENNA INSIDE HER.

DIAPHRAGM

A SMALL FLEXIBLE FRISBEE THAT GETS FILLED WITH SPERMICIDAL CREAM AND INSERTED. TAKE RESPONSIBILITY AND INSERT IT FOR HER. MAKE IT PART OF YOUR FOREPLAY!

CERVICAL CAP

KIND OF LIKE A DIAPHRAGM. STAYS IN LONGER AND NEEDS NO SPERMICIDE. MUST BE CUSTOM-FITTED, LIKE DENTURES. DON'T ASK HOW.

ORAL CONTRACEPTIVES

USUALLY MAKES HER BREASTS BIGGER, WHICH IS MORE FUN FOR YOU. TOO MANY HORMONES AND A DRAG FOR HER. WORKS PERFECT EXCEPT WHEN IT CAUSES CANCER.

GOSSYPOL

THIS IS A MALE BIRTH-CONTROL PILL THAT THEY'RE USING IN CHINA. COULD BE GREAT EXCEPT FOR **ONE** THING...

WITHDRAWAL

NOT A FORM OF BIRTH CONTROL. MAKES YOU NERVOUS AND CAUSES BIG CHANGES IN YOUR LIFE.

Bringing Your Partner to Orgasm

WOMEN OFTEN TAKE MUCH LONGER THAN MEN TO ACHIEVE ORGASM.

HONEY, WHAT DAY IS IT?

THURSDAY—NO, IT'S SATURDAY. MY WATCH STOPPED.

YOU MUST BE GENTLE AND PATIENT...

BUT DARLING, WE'VE BEEN AT THIS SINCE MONDAY NIGHT!

YOU'RE SO SELFISH!

...UNLESS SHE WANTS YOU TO BE A RAGING TIGER...

NO, NO MORE SEX, EVER AGAIN, DO YOU HEAR ME!?

OOH, YOU'RE SO VIRILE WHEN YOU'RE MAD! OK, I'M READY NOW!

BECAUSE OF LOW "ORGASMIC THRESHOLDS," SOME WOMEN RESPOND TO THE SLIGHTEST TOUCH..

GEE, LINDA, I HAD A NICE TIME.

OH-OH-OH!

OTHERS REQUIRE STIMULATION OF A SPECIFIC SMALL AREA.

DOWN AND A LITTLE TO THE LEFT.

THERE?

NO, UP MORE.

THERE?

YEAH, BUT HARDER.

LIKE THIS?

OW! NO. TWIST IT A LITTLE.

TWIST IT?

ALTHOUGH MANY FEEL THAT VERBALLY EXPRESSED SEXUAL REQUESTS RUIN THE SPONTANEITY, IT'S JUST NOT TRUE!

HAVE YOU FINISHED READING THE VIBRATOR MANUAL YET? DID YOU MEMORIZE MY EROGENOUS ZONES? LET ME KNOW WHEN YOU HAVE, OK?

NO. NO. YEAH.

COSMO

DILDO MATIC

Spontaneity KEEPS LOVE ALIVE!

SEXUAL DYSFUNCTION

IT'S QUITE **NORMAL** FOR ANXIETIES TO CREEP UP IN THE MIDDLE OF LOVEMAKING.

OH! OH! OH!

WOMEN'S ANXIETIES CAN BE VERY DIFFERENT FROM MEN'S.

WHAT ARE THOSE BUGS ON MY PHILODENDRON?

WHAT IF THEY DROPPED THE BOMB **RIGHT NOW**?

SOMETIMES, HOWEVER, THEY CAN BE QUITE SIMILAR.

IF I HAD A TRANS-AM, I WOULDN'T HAVE TO **WORRY** ABOUT KEEPING A HARD-ON...

IF I HAD THOSE MAUD FRIZON PUMPS, I'D PROBABLY **ENJOY** DOING THIS...

MOST MATURE WOMEN REALIZE THAT TEMPORARY IMPOTENCE IS **NOT** SERIOUS, AND WILL **TREAT THE MATTER** DELICATELY AND WITH TACT.

CAN'T GET IT UP? IT'S OK, HONEY, WE CAN PLAY "GO FISH" UNTIL YOU'RE IN THE MOOD AGAIN!

NOBODY'S EXPECTING YOU TO **PERFORM**. SOME DAYS ARE JUST NOT GOOD DAYS FOR PENISES.

I'LL BE RIGHT OUT, DARLING!

THERE'S A **REALLY GOOD** TWILIGHT ZONE ON RIGHT **NOW**.

ZITS

WHY DO WOMEN **LOVE** TO SQUEEZE THEIR MATE'S PIMPLES?

OH DARLING!

GET YOUR HANDS OFF THAT ZIT.

WHAT **IS** IT ABOUT SUBCUTANEOUS ERUPTIONS THAT DRIVES WOMEN **WILD?**

OW!

OOH, JUST A LITTLE MORE, HONEY!

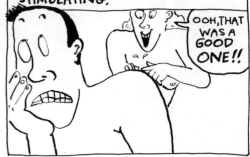

SOME THEORIZE THAT "POPPING A ZIT" SYMBOLIZES A CERTAIN "RELEASE" THAT WOMEN FIND **STIMULATING.**

OOH, THAT WAS A GOOD ONE!!

OTHERS SEE IT AS A NOSTALGIA FOR LOST ADOLESCENCE.

WHO KNOWS? BUT PROPER ETIQUETTE DEMANDS THAT A WOMAN KNOW YOU **AT LEAST** A WEEK BEFORE SHE OFFERS TO "TAKE CARE" OF YOUR PIMPLES.

SAY, BABY, WHUZZAT ON YER NECK THERE? OOOH, COME **CLOSER!**

WHAT A SLUT!

ONE THING IS FOR SURE—IF YOU LOVE HER, YOU'LL LET HER SQUEEZE THEM.

AACK!

OOH, A BLACK-HEAD!

My Secret Shoestore

One Woman's Sexual Fantasy Revealed!

I GO TO BUY A PAIR OF SHOES. THE SALESMAN IS **INCREDIBLY** HANDSOME.

SIZE NINE...MEDIUM...

AN EXCELLENT CHOICE, MODOM.

WHEN HE WATCHES ME SLIP INTO MY "PEDS," I CAN SEE HE IS **AROUSED.**

AS THE SALESMAN FITS ME, HE GETS **CARRIED AWAY.**

CHÉRIE!

WE SPEND THE AFTERNOON LOCKED IN PASSION.

SLINGBACK! DORSAY! PUMP! SPECTATOR! DEMI-BOOT! OH JESUS!

WHEN IT IS TIME FOR ME TO GO, HE GIVES ME THE SHOES AT A 50% DISCOUNT! I HAVE **MULTIPLE ORGASMS.**

R-RING!

$76.99

OH!

??????? ARE YOU Compatible ???????

TAKE THIS SIMPLE QUIZ WITH YOUR GIRLFRIEND OR WIFE TO FIND OUT HOW COMPATIBLE YOU REALLY ARE!

1. WHENEVER I'M LOST, I:
   - (A) GO BACK HOME.
   - (B) FIND A BAR AND FORGET ABOUT MY DESTINATION.

2. (A) I DON'T BELIEVE IN LOVE AT FIRST SIGHT.
   - (B) LET'S FUCK.

3. IF I FOUND A STRAY DOG, I'D SAY:
   - (A) "I KNOW A LAOTIAN REFUGEE FAMILY WHO'RE MIGHTY HUNGRY!"
   - (B) "I JUST TOOK A LAOTIAN COOKING CLASS AND I KNOW THIS GREAT RECIPE!"

4. WHEN I WANT TO HAVE A GOOD TIME, I:
   - (A) SIT AT HOME AND DRINK MYSELF INTO A STUPOR.
   - (B) SIT HOME AND WHACK OFF.

5. (A) I LOVE ENEMAS.
   - (B) I HATE ENEMAS.

6. (A) I HAVE A LOUSY CREDIT RATING.
   - (B) I HAVE 17 CREDIT CARDS, ALL IN OTHER PEOPLE'S NAMES.

7. I PREFER:
   - (A) TUINOLS
   - (B) BENZEDRINE

8. MY GOALS IN LIFE INCLUDE:
   - (A) GETTING OUT OF BED.
   - (B) GOING DOWN TO THE CORNER TO GET A PACK OF CIGARETTES.

9. MY IDEA OF EXPERIMENTING SEXUALLY IS:
   - (A) LETTING YOU GET ON TOP.
   - (B) ON TOP OF WHAT?

10. WHEN I UNDRESS BEFORE GOING TO BED, I:
   - (A) MAKE SURE I CAN FIND THE SAME CLOTHES IN THE MORNING TO PUT ON AGAIN.
   - (B) UNDRESS?

Answers to this quiz appear nowhere in this book!

HOW YOU CAN TELL IF SHE'S *In Love* WITH YOU

WEARS A SLACK-JAWED EXPRESSION.

LIKES **ALL** YOUR FRIENDS.

DOESN'T CARE A **FIG** ABOUT YOUR LITTLE FAULTS.

IS EAGER TO DO FAVORS FOR YOU.

BELIEVES YOU WHEN YOU LIE.

LAUGHS AT ALL YOUR JOKES.

Buying Lingerie

MANY MEN WOULD LOVE TO BUY THOSE SEXY LITTLE UNDERGARMENTS FOR THEIR PARAMOURS— BUT THEY JUST DON'T KNOW **HOW**...

IT CAN BE AN AWKWARD TASK.

WELL, HONEY, IS SHE ABOUT **MY** SIZE?

WELL, NO, I MEAN, YES— I MEAN SORT OF— UM, I THINK I FORGOT MY CHESTBOOK— I MEAN, MY CHECKBOOK...

FOR SOME REASON, YOU FEEL LIKE YOU'VE BEEN CAUGHT DOING SOMETHING **BAD**.

SOMETHING I CAN HELP YOU WITH, **YOUNG MAN**?

NO! HONEST!

THERE'S NO GETTING AWAY FROM THE FACT THAT YOU **ARE** THINKING DIRTY THOUGHTS.

YES SIR, SHOPPING FOR THOSE SKIMPY LITTLE THINGS CAN GET YOU INTO **BIG TROUBLE**.

PERHAPS YOU'D BE INTERESTED IN SEEING OUR **DELUXE** SELECTION.

B-B-B-B-BU-BU-BU- SURE!

TRY TO KEEP YOUR PERSPECTIVE ON THE ECONOMICS INVOLVED.

ALL RIGHT SIR. THAT COMES TO $788.69. I HOPE YOU... ENJOY IT.

SURE YOU BET HECK!

$788.69

THE TELL-TALE SIGNS

YOU CAN OFTEN TELL BY SUBTLE SIGNALS THAT YOUR MATE IS SUFFERING FROM PRE-MENSTRUAL TENSION— HERE ARE JUST A FEW!

SHE BEGINS TO CRY IF YOU...

HONEY?

OHHHHH!

ASK HER IF SHE WANTS A TUNA SANDWICH.

SHE BEGINS TO SOB HYSTERICALLY IF YOU...

BOOHOOHO HOOHOOHO HOOBOOHO

HONEY?

ASK HER HOW HER DAY WAS.

SHE CRAWLS INTO A FETAL POSITION WHEN YOU...

DEAR, ALL I SAID WAS THAT YOU LOOKED LOVELY.

COMPLIMENT HER.

FIGHTING IN PUBLIC

DIRECT CONFRONTATION IS A GOOD WAY TO SOLVE PROBLEMS.

BOY, THIS CHICKEN IS **GREAT**! TOO BAD **DARLA** HERE CAN'T COOK LIKE THIS!

IT HELPS TO CLEAR THE AIR AND MAKE YOUR RELATIONSHIP STRONGER.

OH YEAH? WELL MAYBE IF YOU WERE COOKING IN THE **BEDROOM**, I'D BE COOKING IN THE KITCHEN!

INTERNALIZING YOUR ANGER IS AN UNHEALTHY THING TO DO, SO...

WELL, IF WE SCREWED MORE THAN **ONCE A MONTH** MAYBE I'D HAVE MORE PRACTICE!

WHY YOU...

I'LL GET **DESSERT**.

IF YOU TELL A FRIEND HOW YOU FEEL FIRST, IT CAN HELP YOU ARTICULATE YOUR PROBLEM TO YOUR MATE,

WE **DON'T** SCREW BECAUSE HE **CAN'T**!

NEED **HELP**, DEAR?

GRRR...

FRIENDS CAN HELP YOU BY PROVIDING A NEW PERSPECTIVE ON YOUR RELATIONSHIP.

IF **SHE** WASN'T SUCH A **BALLBUSTER**—

IF **HE** WASN'T SUCH A **WIMP**—HELEN? ROY?

SOMETIMES ANALYZING OTHERS' RELATIONSHIPS CAN HELP YOURS, TOO!

HEY! THEY'RE **GONE**!

GEE. HOW ODD. DID YOU NOTICE HOW **TENSE** THEY BOTH SEEMED? I THINK THEY'RE HAVING **SEX** PROBLEMS.

How To **BREAK UP** With A Woman

YOU AWAKEN ONE MORNING TO REALIZE **SHE** IS NOT THE WOMAN OF YOUR DREAMS.

ZZZZ

HOW TO EXTRICATE YOURSELF, DELICATELY AND SENSITIVELY?

"JUST GOING OUT TO GET A PACK OF CIGARETTES?" NO, **THAT** WON'T WORK...

EVERY WOMAN HAS ALREADY HEARD **THIS** PHRASE:

OH MURIEL... YOU'RE **TOO GOOD** FOR ME!

THEN GET YOUR FACE OUT OF MY TITS.

IT'S UP TO YOU TO SAY SOMETHING TACTFUL AND SENSITIVE.

OH DARLING DEBBIE. THERE'S SOMETHING I NEED TO TELL YOU.

YES, DEAR?

I'M TOO **GOOD** FOR YOU.

YOU SEE, DEBBIE, I FINALLY REALIZED THAT **I** AM GOD'S GIFT TO WOMEN.

Continued

... continued from previous page

SO, YOU SEE, IT WOULD BE **UNFAIR** OF YOU TO KEEP ME TO YOURSELF...

SO I WAS HOPING YOU **WOULDN'T MIND** PROVIDING ME WITH A LIST OF ALL YOUR GIRLFRIENDS' PHONE NUMBERS, ESPECIALLY **JUDY**, THE BLONDE.

OF COURSE, WITH ANY BREAK-UP, THERE IS THE **BITTERSWEET**...

JUST THINK, DARLING. YOUR FRIENDS CAN HAVE WHAT **WE** HAVE SHARED.

USE THIS LAST LINE AT **YOUR OWN RISK**.

OF COURSE, I HOPE THAT WE CAN STILL BE FRIENDS...

BE PREPARED TO DODGE FLYING PROJECTILES.

...LET'S HAVE LUNCH SOON!

MYSTIC Wedding Shower Rituals REVEALED!

WHAT MEN INNOCENTLY THINK IS A SIMPLE "HEN PARTY..."

I'M OFF TO CINDY'S SHOWER, HONEY, BYE-BYE!

HAVE FUN, DEAR! HEH-HEH...

...IS ACTUALLY A DARK **SAVAGE RITE** OF WOMANHOOD!

ARE YOU READY, **O WORTHLESS ONE**?

THE BRIDE-TO-BE IS "SHOWERED" WITH A **NUBILE SURFER YOUTH.**

LOWER THE NUPTIAL SURROGATE!

OOH!

THE LIGHTS GO DOWN AND AN **UNDULATING** MELODY COMES OUT OF NOWHERE, MASKING THE SOUND OF **FLESH ON FLESH.**

What happens next I cannot disclose. Fear of recrimination from the ancient "shower sect" seals my lips...

JUST DON'T LAUGH THE NEXT TIME SOMEONE **YOU** KNOW ATTENDS A SHOWER...

HAVE FUN, DEAR?

SMECK!

OH YES. CINDY JUST **LOVED** THE SALAD CRUETS. DARLA BAKED THE **CUTEST** CAKE...

PRE-NUPTIAL NIGHTMARE

EVERY GROOM INVOLVED IN A WEDDING, LARGE OR SMALL, SHOULD BE PREPARED FOR THE **TRAVAILS OF BETROTHAL.**

YOUR OPINION **WILL** BE ASKED,

NOW HONEY, ARE YOU GOING TO HAVE MINTS OR JORDAN ALMONDS?

I LIKE JORDAN ALMONDS - WHAT DO **YOU** THINK, DEAR?

IT'S IMPORTANT TO BE EXTREMELY **DIPLOMATIC.**

HM? I DON'T CARE.

YOU DON'T **CARE?**

CALL OFF THE WEDDING, DEAR. I DON'T WANT YOU MARRYING THIS **THOUGHTLESS SLOB!**

IT'S USUALLY BEST TO SIMPLY LET THE BRIDE AND HER FAMILY DO WHAT THEY WANT.

SO MOTHER AND I THOUGHT PINK FOR THE BRIDESMAIDS AND LIME GREEN TUXES FOR THE USHERS SOUNDED **WONDERFUL.** DON'T YOU THINK SO?

GREAT, DEAR...

AVOID ARGUMENTS. THERE'S **ENOUGH** STRESS AS IT IS.

WHAT? NO FRIENDS OF MINE WOULD BE CAUGHT **DEAD IN** LIME GREEN!

BUT I ALREADY ORDERED THEM! THOSE ARE OUR **THEME COLORS** TO CHERISH **FOREVER**-BOOHOOHOOHOO

ABOVE ALL, REMEMBER: IT'S NOT REALLY YOUR WEDDING - IT'S **HER MOTHER'S.**

TO HAVE AND TO HOLD,...

TO HAVE AND TO HOLD,...

TO HAVE AND TO HOLD,...